Ann ~

Thank you for your friendship ~ we hope you will come visit us in St. Augustine / Villano Beach !

Love ~
Terri and
Roger

July 2016

# Floridanos, Menorcans, Cattle-Whip Crackers

# Poetry of St. Augustine

*HB Masters*

Ann Browning Masters

FLORIDANOS, MENORCANS, CATTLE-WHIP CRACKERS
POETRY OF ST. AUGUSTINE

Cover design by Jon White

ISBN 13: 978-1-886104-77-8

The Florida Historical Society Press
435 Brevard Avenue
Cocoa, FL 32922
http://myfloridahistory.org/fhspress

P•R•E•S•S

# Publishing Acknowledgments

My thanks to the editors of the following publications in which these poems previously appeared:

*Ancient City Poets, Authors, Photographers, and Artists Literary Magazine*, Poet Plant Press: "Hurricane";

*The 2014 Marjorie Kinnan Rawlings Journal of Florida Literature:* "We Are Menorcans," "Thelma Padgett's Home Across From the Methodist Church," "Summer Dark Porch-Sitting Nights," "Into the Neighborhood," "Paul Victor, December 1941," "Old City Divorce," "Widger and Waukie and Me," "Johnny Mae Kept Us, But Plessy Had Us All," "Three Years Later: Marineland, Summer 1967";

*The 2011 Marjorie Kinnan Rawlings Journal of Florida Literature:* "Stout Wood, Heart Wood," "We Ain't Scufflin'," "Is There a Wine?," "The St. Augustine Menorcan Litmus Test," "Elegy for the Children of Henry and Agnes Sanchez";

*Kalliope*: "Hurricane Lady," "Miss Rita Masters' Grocery," "Nana Explains Life and Death";

*Jacksonville Success Guide* (now *Arbus*): "Home by Dark," "Elegy for the Children of Henry and Agnes Sanchez";

*My Shameless St. Augustine Scrapbook*, ed. by Ruth Moon Kempher: "You Want Mullet?";

*The Second Friends of the Frogs Anthology*, ed. by Ruth Moon Kempher: "How Can I Move Here?," "Saint October," "You Want Mullet?"

Thanks also to the editor of the St. Augustine Historical Society 2007 Journal of History, *El Escribano*, in which a narrative excerpt from this book appeared.

# Dedication

This is for Forrest, the boy who asked,
"Do you realize you've talked about dead people for two hours?"

# List of Illustrations

# Table of Contents

# Publisher's Note

Established in 1856, the Florida Historical Society (FHS) is an independent not-for-profit entity dedicated to educating the public about the rich history and culture of our diverse state. Publishing is at the heart of the Florida Historical Society mission. The Florida Historical Society began publishing our outstanding academic journal the *Florida Historical Quarterly* in 1908. Since 1925, the Florida Historical Society has been publishing books, beginning with the *History of Jacksonville, Florida and Vicinity* by T. Frederick Davis. For 78 years, the FHS only occasionally published books, but in 2003, the decision was made to establish a more active and regular publication schedule. Today, the Florida Historical Society Press is publishing between five and ten books per year.

The Florida Historical Society Press preserves Florida's past through the publication of books on a wide variety of topics relating to our state's diverse history and culture. We publish non-fiction books, of course, and our goal of disseminating Florida history to the widest possible audience is also well served by the publication of novels firmly based upon scholarly research. Teachers and students alike find that our high quality fictionalized accounts of Florida history bring the past to life and make historic events, people and places more accessible and "real." We also publish books focusing on creative expressions of Florida history and culture such as painting, cooking, and photography.

*Floridanos, Menorcans, Cattle-Whip Crackers: Poetry of St. Augustine* by Ann Browning Masters is our first collection of poems related to Florida history. We feel that Dr. Masters' poetry presents particular aspects of Florida history from a personal perspective that adds depth to our understanding of what it is like to be a part of the St. Augustine community, both past and present. Her insights are particularly relevant as we commemorate the 450th anniversary of the establishment of St. Augustine. We hope you enjoy and are enriched by this work.

Dr. Ben Brotemarkle
Executive Director
Florida Historical Society
April 2015

# Acknowledgments

I am grateful for the opportunity to grow up in St. Augustine and for knowing my Floridano/Menorcan/Cracker family and community. Writing this book has been an experience of standing on their shoulders.

A special thanks is given to Sandra Parks for her mentorship and suggestion that I submit my manuscript to the Florida Historical Society for consideration. I am forever grateful for her vision and good cheer. FHS Executive Director Dr. Ben Brotemarkle has patiently shepherded my work through the publication process, and I am indebted to him for sound guidance and insights I would not have developed on my own. I appreciate the skill of copy editor Christine Gallaway, who made a valuable contribution to the style and form of this book. And thanks to Jon White, the designer of this wonderful book cover, for capturing an icon of St. Augustine that speaks to the heart of my work.

The St. Augustine Historical Society Research Library staff has been very important in the background development of this book. I am indebted to Leslie Wilson, Judith Foxworth, Charles Tingley, and Bob Nawrocki. Thanks is also given to Myron Kirkus of the Jacksonville Public Library, Dr. Christina Will and Royce Bass of the St. Johns River State College Library, and archivists Sister Thomas Joseph McGoldrick, SSJ, and Sister Catherine Bitzer, SSJ.

I have appreciated comments and feedback from Professors Nona Mitchell Asconi, Michael Crocker, Mark Little, Susan Ross, Sandie Stratton, and Roger Vaccaro. Drs. Patricia Griffin, Susan Parker, and Barbara Wingo have been of great assistance in providing historical and cultural clarity. Early critiques from Peter Meinke were very helpful in my literary focus. I have appreciated Lola Haskins' support in the time she has given to share her understanding and exaltation of Old Florida.

Fernando Serrano Llabres and the late Dr. Victoriano Seoane-Pascucci have provided insights on life in Menorca before and after the Menorcan colony migrated to the New World. Their interest in contemporary St. Augustine Menorcan-Americans has helped to illustrate the continuing thread of Old World connections found in this book.

I am also indebted to Carol Lopez Bradshaw, Barbara Usina Jones, Herbie Greenleaf, Sandy Usina Nester, Gracie Delany Cothron, Donald Crichlow, Cecil Pacetti, Ralph and Florence Powers, Donna Campbell Swan, Theresa Campbell Grady, Sharon Campbell Browning, and Kathy Campbell McKenna for sharing their memories and providing me with materials used in this book. I beg forgiveness from other good souls who have helped in this work and whose names I have temporarily missed.

Friday evenings with my mother, Shirley Sanchez Browning, have been a great joy and help in clarifying details of my research. I have appreciated the listening support of my sister, Cecile Browning Nusbaum, and the early writing advice of my brother, James Browning.

I am deeply grateful to Barbara Barker, Marguerite and Jim Diffin, and Sandra Nelson, members of my long-time writing critique group. This group's expertise, clear eye, perfect ear, and patience of Job continually raised the standard of this manuscript and helped me to say what I really wanted to say. They have been my touchstone for over 30 years.

My son, Forrest, gave me the impetus to begin this book. One evening in the late 1980s we visited my husband's grandparents, and laughed, gossiped, and reminisced about old times and dear faces. I was completely unaware of our almost-teenager son's boredom until, as we were getting in the car to go home, he asked what I now think of as *the question*.

No, I didn't realize that I had talked about dead people for two hours that evening. All the departed that we recalled were alive to me. Some of them had not been alive during my lifetime; others had passed before I was alert enough to understand their memories had passage to times a hundred years ago. But, in my mind, I knew their stories, ways, streets and roads, and the emotional and social order in which they lived. I knew the lay of the land and the timbre of their lives in St. Augustine and St. Johns

County from after the Civil War to the Civil Rights Movement that began in my teens.

And I want my son to be able to remember these moments, the real ones and the folk traditions that have been passed down. So I have gathered the richness of stories about common people and common life. I want to share them with the world, but I especially leave them for my son, Forrest, to remember.

Without the support and encouragement from my husband, Jeremy Masters, this book could not have been completed. I owe a special debt to his technical assistance, ability to keep the home front at bay for me, and pitch-perfect feedback on Floridano/Menorcan/Cracker life. He has been my boon companion in this endeavor, and, for living through it with me, will always have my deepest gratitude.

# Introduction

Some of our families have been in St. Augustine for over 400 years. Some of our families drove over the Bridge of Lions for the first time four minutes ago. Regardless of when we arrived, many of us are so captivated with St. Augustine that we never want to leave, even when that same drawbridge makes us late or has us up in arms with each other about what to do with it.

I am a native St. Augustinian, and I am fascinated with a sliver of St. Augustine time that began nine decades before my birth. I am also a lover of the poetry here that sings through the lives of common folks. This is why I want to tell you about an era that started during the Civil War and ended in the 1980s. It was bound south by Moultrie Creek, west by Holy Branch, east by the Atlantic Ocean, and by the North City Gates. It is an immigrant, generational story of plain folk, not First Spanish Period Dons or Henry Flagler's gilded players. Many of its people and much of its language have become memories that are so ephemeral they may be lost to the generation after me.

I grew up knowing that St. Augustine was a special place to live. Before it became a political slogan, an earlier generation commented on their childhood and early adulthood from time to time, saying that "people were kinder back then." Maybe people seemed kinder because the community knew itself. In church or synagogue you would see the shop owner, the grocer, the school teacher, the farmer, and you knew you would see them again during the week. The grocery delivery boy understood that his livelihood depended on maintaining a tactful amnesia for whatever he saw when coming in the back door.

But that kindness was circumscribed by race, religion, when one's family moved to the county, and into whose family one married. There was, therefore, no anonymous crowd from which cruel acts could be brazenly committed. Any victims certainly knew their tormentors.

My generation was also touched by this communal knowledge. Residents during my youth may not have spoken to, agreed with, or courted all of their fellow citizens, but they knew each other. My grandfather got right to the heart of it if he didn't recognize the young suitor on his couch. He said it directly: "Who's your daddy, son?"

This sense of connectedness still binds many of us together. I recognize this on Friday evenings when my husband and I have dinner with my mother and we spend an hour placing the third generation of a maiden name to its last two households. I want to preserve this sense of place. I want to ensure a continuation of the spoken knowledge about St. Augustine and St. Johns County.

My version of this time period, however, represents a pre-memory and memory of the people and situations around me and is not representative of every lived experience of the time. Some of the oral traditions are stories made up and embellished by the tellers, passed along in years long gone, changed eventually by a telephone game's repetition. Some known-for-a-fact events are occasionally described differently by two different Floridanos, Menorcans, or Crackers. The poetry of place sings here, but not always with the same words for everyone.

Ultimately, these narrative poems are a convergence of deep España with the deep South, a second chapter of passionate Menorcan determination that melded into a Cracker landscape. They reflect an infusion of beliefs, faiths, and cultures that have simmered, and sometimes roiled, for over a hundred years; of civil wrongs before there was hope for civil rights. They speak the patois of Floridanos and Menorcans, of Cracker children taught by French and Irish Catholic Sisters, of northern accents gone to a native twang, and a melodious distillation of Mediterranean cadence. You may yet hear this to-the-heart conversation in St. Augustine.

# In St. Augustine, Land of Flowers, Who Were Floridanos, Menorcans, Cattle-Whip Crackers?

### First Spanish Period: 1565 - 1763

Spanish citizens born in St. Augustine were recorded as "Floridanos" in the census sent to Spain.

### British Period: 1764 - 1784

Several Floridano men remained in St. Augustine during the British period, but most Floridanos went to Cuba and Spain.

In 1777, indentured servants, mostly from the Balearic island of Menorca, Italy, and Greece, walked to St. Augustine from the failed indigo plantation of Scottish Dr. Andrew Turnbull. This group of Roman Catholics and Greek Orthodox eventually became known as Menorcans in St. Augustine.

### Second Spanish Period: 1784 - 1821

Some Floridanos returned to St. Augustine from Cuba, Spain, and other Spanish holdings. Menorcans remained in St. Augustine after the British Period ended. Intermarriage between Floridanos and Menorcans began during this period.

### U.S. Territorial Period: 1821 - 1845
### U.S. Statehood: 1845

Some Scots-Irish and English American settlers who became known as Crackers entered Florida, and a trickle of their marriages to Floridano-Menorcans and Menorcans began.

### Twentieth-Century St. Augustine:

Anthropologist Dr. Patricia Griffin, an expert on the colonial Menorcan experience, stated that Thalassemia, a disease common to Mediterraneans (including Menorcans), has decreased with increased exogamous marriages by Menorcans. She reported that, "In spite of these marriages the 'Minorcans' remained remarkably inbred until the beginning of the twentieth century....At present the group is gradually being assimilated into the general population. A newspaper survey for 1974-1975 yielded the information that only one of four marriages was contracted between 'pure line' (as identified by genealogical information) Minorcans." (p. 15)

### An Example of a Floridano-Menorcan Family With Parents Born in Spanish Florida, Children Born in U.S. Territorial Florida and U.S. Florida

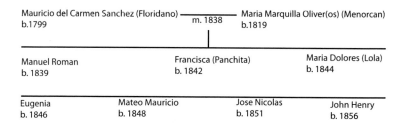

Incorrect information taken from Confederate writings after the Civil War identifies Mauricio Sanchez as an "old Cuban." This inaccuracy has been perpetuated in some contemporary electronic data collections. Cathedral Parish records of St. Augustine indicate that he was born, baptized, and married in St. Augustine.

# I  Floridanos

# And Some Were Spies

Francisca (Panchita), Maria Dolores (Lola), and Eugenia San-chez were Floridanas-Menorcans. They were also Confederate spies during the Civil War. Unfortunately, their ailing and aged father, Mauricio, was mistaken for the person passing Union intelligence to the Confederacy, and was imprisoned in the Union-held Castillo de San Marcos.

One evening Lola, Eugenia, and Panchita* overheard battle plans while they appeased Union soldiers with dinner prepara-tions. Prompted by this information, Lola made a wild ride to the St. Johns River and borrowed a rowboat to cross to Confederate lines. This probably would not have been possible without her sisters' hair-raising resourcefulness as they cooked dinner and hid her departure from the Union soldiers.

Initial reports claimed that Lola rowed across the wide St. Johns River, but Carol Lopez Bradshaw and others think that she crossed a smaller tributary or creek to arrive at Captain Dicki-son's† Camp Davis. All chronicles agree that Lola was clever enough to leave the lathered horse far away from the farmhouse when she returned. Lola's ride resulted in a Confederate victory. For this, and other intelligence gathering that she and her sisters provided, a captured Union pontoon boat was re-named *Three Sisters*.


*Francesca was affectionately known as Panchita. Lola's grand-niece Shirley Sanchez Browning remembers her Sanchez uncles referring to Francesca as Aunt 'Chita.

†His name has also been reported as Dickenson in the St. Ambrose Parish history.

# Lola Sanchez:

*Floridanos, Menorcans, Cattle-Whip Crackers*

Yes, I did leave Eugenia
and Panchita in the kitchen
to bluff-hungry Union boys.
And I rode like a woman-fool
to the river, to the Johnny soldiers
who launched my boat and all their stories.
This was all we knew: spy-parley, flight.
*Young women don't picture being hanged.*
When their boys re-name a beaten-down
Yankee barque *Three Sisters,* they smile,
they curtsy. They think they ride a history,
but it does not step where they thought.

History could join up again
like creek branches, Papá said.
The old Floridano, after all, had
married my Menorquina Mamá.
Then they watched a herd of wars
dance like wild-eyed horses
across the peninsula. They knew
being any Rebel could be temporary.
"Another battle," he said, "another
treaty, *hablamos español.*"
They were not here, merciful God
to mourn the next war – with Spain.

History wrote its own book,
without our name. Sweet Mother,
who remembers when this new world
began to sliver change among us?
I have children, and children's children,
and now they are called  *Crackers*?

For whips! For American cattle! As if
Spanish cows never left the boats!
Listen, child. Hold this tight: Grandpapá's
*abuelo* fetched our first herd, taught us
how to work them, passed down his heart.
This is how we bore all the Floridas,
bred and raised all the bloodlines:
these Floridanos, these Menorcans,
these cattle-whip Crackers.

*hablamos español:* pronounced ah-blah-mose esp-spahn-yol; we speak Spanish
*abuelo:*   pronounced ah-bway-low; grandfather

Menorcans: Descendants from Dr. Andrew Turnbull's 18th century indigo plan-
    tation in New Smyrna, south of St. Augustine. Colonists were recruited
    from Italy, Greece, and Spain's Balearic island of Menorca (then a Brit-
    ish possession) to become indentured servants on the plantation. After
    years of ill-treatment and failure to be released after contracts had
    been served, the colony walked to then-British St. Augustine and was
    given asylum in 1777 by the British Governor. Intermarriage while the
    colonists waited to be transported from Menorca to Florida, and inter-
    marriage ever since, has resulted in the name Menorcan often being
    used to describe the entire population.

The British spelling Minorcan was originally used to describe this population in
St. Augustine. Recently, though, many of these descendants refer to themselves
using the Spanish spelling Menorcan.

Cracker: There are many origins for this term, varying over place and time. For
    some, it has come to be synonymous for being a bigot. For others, it is
    embraced as emblematic of pioneer farming and ranching heritage. In
    most cases in this book, the term refers to the historically fiercely inde-
    pendent, poor Southerners who lived as self-sufficiently as possible on
    the land. The origin usage in this book, in all cases but one (*Vernon
    and Moses Tell It at the Depot*), is of people who cracked whips while
    herding cattle.

1889 Jacksonville, Tampa, Key West Railway Connection System map, with permission of St. Augustine Historical Society

# Stout Wood, Heart Wood

In 1903 the Clyde Steamship Company map of Florida presented steamship routes and railroad connections. One of the rail connections was Holy Branch, a very small farming community twenty miles west of St. Augustine and just east of the relatively new town of Hastings. A small creek called Holy Branch then ran through the Sanchez family homestead, built in 1883 by John Henry Sanchez, youngest brother of Lola Sanchez.

Holy Branch is not on the map now. It has become Spuds, which is a fitting name for potato and cabbage country.

The old Sanchez farm was visited regularly by the St. Ambrose Parish priest, Father Stephen Langlade. In the centennial history of St. Ambrose Parish, a story of Father Langlade's love for his parish is revealed. When the Bishop issued a transfer order, Father Langlade disobeyed the order. He took off his collar and sat in the front pew at Mass, to the discomfort of the substitute priest sent from St. Augustine. Father Langlade repented and the Bishop finally relented. Father Langlade did penance and served his beloved parish for forty-nine years.

When asked about the origin of the name Holy Branch, a Menorcan woman, whose name is lost to the many years gone of my youth, said, "Well, they were a very religious family, you know."

# Stout Wood, Heart Wood

Stout wood. Heart wood.
First time right nails.
Henry Sanchez in a clearing
built a homestead by the quail's
path, creek's bath, moccasin trails.

Had potatoes in the ground
after oranges on the tree;
put the boys in saddles
to work the cattle. He
fiddled like a Cracker
when the crop was done;
had the priest to stay
on his weekly run.

Well dippin', egg pickin'
Agnes, by his side,
put cabbage in jars,
baked sweet potato pie,
raised a clutch of children
on the Holy Branch land:
three hundred acres of the
Spanish king's sand.

Pioneers from hard work,
mosquito bites, and heat,
Sanchez children lived on pilau,
gopher stew, and smokehouse meat;
made their prayers in the morning,
told their beads at night,
rode the buggy to St. Ambrose
to keep their Sunday right.

Stout wood. Heart wood.
Timbered and lathed.
Holy Branch children saw God
in the seasons of each green blade,
plowed straight, tended calves, and prayed.

pilau: pronounced pearl-low; a tomato-roux-based rice dish that includes a
small amount of meat or seafood

gopher stew: a stew made from the gopher land tortoise. (Gophers are now on
the endangered species list and this stew is no longer legally tasted in
St. Augustine.)

# The Sanchez Ghosts' Lament
# for Annie Laurie

For many years country marriages (meaning any west of Dixie Highway or as far away as Plumb Nelly*) usually occurred between folks of the same religion. And if they didn't share the same pew before they were married, they most often did after marriage.

In the 1920s, hard-shell Baptist Annie Laurie Ivey arrived from Georgia to visit her uncle Byron Ivey in Elkton, a farming community near Holy Branch. Mr. Ivey owned a country store in Elkton and there he employed Charley Sanchez (son of Henry and Agnes Sanchez).

Charley soon courted Annie Laurie. After they married, he took her home to his enduring and extended family of the cradle-Catholic variety. What followed can only be described as all parties clinging to their faith.

Annie Laurie, however, was outnumbered, and suffered more than the usual indignities heaped on in-laws from outside the tightly knit community. Since they're all in heaven now, a revisionist history can speculate that the Sanchez ghosts of Holy Branch sing a lament for her sorrows.

*Plumb Nelly: plumb out of town and nearly (nelly) out of the county

# The Sanchez Ghosts' Lament
# for Annie Laurie

*Hard-shell Baptist Annie Laurie Ivey went up in there amongst those cradle-Catholics at Holy Branch and married Charley Sanchez. She was outnumbered and outflanked from day one. —*
*Anonymous relative*

Forgive our ways, dear Annie Laurie.
We truly thought that we were right.
This was our home a hundred years.
We had our pride. We had our might.

Forgive our ways, dear Annie Laurie,
for they were harsh and clannish ways.
Ought should live as then you did
in your new and married days.

Forgive our ways, dear Annie Laurie,
so fair and brave, unlike our own.
We did not know to give much care
to one so far away from home.

Forgive our ways, dear Annie Laurie,
blue-eyed bride whom we gave pain.
If only we could bid you love,
or time could bring you here again.

If only we could bid you love,
or time could bring you here again.

Photographs of oak canopy road that leads to St. Ambrose Church and Cemetery: c. 1895, with permission of Sandie A. Stratton; 2015, with permission of Jeremy A. Masters

# Elegy for the Children of Henry and Agnes Sanchez

Don Jose Sanchez de Ortigosa came to St. Augustine from Ronda, Spain, in 1713. In 1714 he married Juana Perez, a local Spanish woman whose St. Augustine maternal ancestors from 1602* on had made a habit of marrying non-native St. Augustine Spaniards like him.

John Henry Sanchez (b. 1856) was the ninth generation of the 1602 family line. He was the son of Floridano Mauricio Sanchez and Menorcan Maria Oliveros. He was also youngest brother to his Confederate spy sisters. The year after the Civil war ended, when Henry was ten years old, his mother died. According to his granddaughter, Shirley Sanchez Browning, he was then raised by sister Lola Sanchez, and lived with Lola and Emanuel Lopez after they wed in 1868. His residence with them has been documented in the 1870 Florida Census.

In 1883 Henry married Agnes Severina Weedman, daughter of Paul Lucian Weidman/Weedman and Menorcana Antonia Josephine Rogero. Henry and Agnes raised nine children at Holy Branch. The Sanchez family farmed a large variety of crops, raised cattle, and kept strong ties with the St. Ambrose Parish. They were especially close to St. Ambrose's founding priest, tee-totaling Father Stephen Langlade.

The Sanchez family lived in the New World first as Floridanos in a Spanish colony, as Floridano-Menorcans in British Florida and the Second Spanish Period, as Americans after 1821, and then as Johnny Rebs. After the Civil War and Florida's re-entry into the Union, they continued to raise cattle and farm at Holy Branch as the family had done in Northeast Florida since Spanish colonial days.

*This is the betrothal/marriage of Diego Alvarez and Elena Gonzalez

# Elegy for the Children of Henry and Agnes Sanchez

Afraid to leave the graveyard
where a little less history waits outside,
we tell stories by stones named for us.
The lap of St. Ambrose Cemetery shifts
to hold another pioneer child come home.

The fair brings them back, spring
blinking away a quarter-second of funeral time.
Preacher Triay thumps his ladle, yells "Gopher stew!"
A backbone of women pile, heap, mound pilau;
new blooded maidens snap their rags full
to impudence, swiping away our crumbs.
Outside men step a beer-hiding shuffle;
Father Langlade's forgotten choreography slides on.

The quick and the dead catch hands on the oak path
from cemetery to church hall on fair day.
Hattie's laughter moves through new babies and
arches in the canopy of a Spanish moss lane.
Charley watches great-grands flay the go-fish pond,
naming their names until the quiet one feels the love
of his breath and smiles into the pulling shadow,
knowing from the light that falls between trees
whose children will next play on bare cedar roots.

We have got shut their faith, yet fret
after the polestars who loved us.
Hanging back for an hour of Cracker comfort
to ease the gate click, we make epic
common folk uncommonly determined
to burn home fires through a scrub night.

19

# A Dream of Passing at Holy Branch

In the past, a long, tree-lined lane led to the old Sanchez home-site. As was customary to help avoid the spread of fire, a roofed dog trot separated the kitchen from the main house. The Floridano-Menorcan homestead resembled what many today might think of as a Cracker-style setting.

The old citrus orchard is gone, there is no cow to be milked, and the cistern is dry. But if you had passed through the lane in the early 20th century, you could peer through shrubbery and expect to see someone throwing scratch to the chickens or checking on new calves waiting in the pasture.

# A Dream of Passing at Holy Branch

Granddaddy sits as he did in life,
on a buckboard down the lane's end.
He motions me down the tree-lined rut.
Should I leave? Should I go with him?

Some nights the dead walk living ground
and turn to me, smiling. I have found
I sleep in their bed, then wake in their mind.
Let's cut-the-fool, drink grape-arbor wine,
eat fat peanuts from salt-water brine,
and come back, come back, one more time.

Bed by the window on full moon nights
I've seen the same unearthly light
illumine the pecan, the pear, the fence.
When through the screen came jasmine air
and horse stall snorts, though Paint's not there,
I have dreamed how it felt to step free.

We will *all* come back to Holy Branch,
if just for these owl nights in June.
The land and the oaks and the bourbony creek
sing the names from our birthing rune.
Should I leave? Should I go with him?
The happy dead say *Get up. Climb in.*

# II Menorcans

# Menorcans

In her *Cross Creek Cookery*, Marjorie Kinnan Rawlings describes how, in 1768, Andrew Turnbull brought indentured servants from Italy, Greece, and the Balearic Island of Menorca, near Spain, to work on his plantation at present day New Smyrna, Florida. She claimed that Turnbull treated the group, now collectively known as Menorcans, as slaves.

After the Menorcans were released from Turnbull's rule by the British Governor, most settled in St. Augustine. In 1784, they welcomed the returning Floridanos and new Spanish settlers when Spain controlled Florida again. Although many Menorcans were still working their way out of financial ruin, they co-existed comfortably, in worship and marriage, with their better-off Spanish cousins.

At the end of the 19th century and beginning of the 20th century, some non-Spanish newcomers to St. Augustine saw the Menorcans differently. Historian Thomas Graham in *The Awakening of St. Augustine* says that ". . . well-meaning gentlemen might contrast "decent society" with "the Minorcans," and coarser men in the ranks of [Anglo] newcomers would disparage the natives as "Turnbull's Negroes."

Historian Sandie A. Stratton casts some light on the pall of prejudice that was sometimes directed toward Menorcans through the 20th century. She states "I think one of the reasons this "Turnbull's Niggers" slur persists is part of a larger trend to deny the presence and legitimacy of the history of indentured servitude in this country. I think the impact and importance of indentured servitude, especially during the 18th century in the U.S., is poorly understood, and thought of by many as embarrassing or derogatory."

# We Are Menorcans

We were called "Turnbull's niggers."
That is still a hard thing to say.
Some of us remember that name,
others recall only the smirk
when we said Menorcan.
But we are strong and proud
and we have survived more
than lack of social standing.

When Daddy's cousin Mercedes
calls about the old, old pictures,
we bleed a little, though, over what
we can't put in words to children
who want to shop the mall.
"What if she dies next week?" I say.
They do not know that if they miss
this visit, they miss their place in time.
They have become white Americans.
They assume that we always were.

Once we were second-class and free.
We owned our Sunday afternoons.
It was disrespectful to God,
crazy, for Menorcans with time
to fritter it away from family.
We were comforted by
the trinity of fused onion,
tomatoes, green peppers,
glad for the datil pepper bite
that said "We are alive!"

We are Menorcans who remember
joy when the roof didn't leak.
Mercedes' poor husband knows all this.

Non-Menorcan, yet he windmills
along US1, trying to bring her home.
None of us live there any more,
but we like to visit. We like
to bring our children with us.


datil pepper: pronounced dat´(like fat)-till; a very hot, slightly sweet, pepper
  grown in the St. Augustine area, often used to season local dishes such
  as pilau

Photograph of Silidonio and Urbana Aguiar Pellicer c. 1880, with permission of Donna Campbell Swan

# Home by Dark

Carl Canova (1882-1957) suddenly went blind in the St. Augustine Plaza-bay front area. According to grand-niece Barbara Usina Jones, "He was a fisherman and one day after lifting a heavy anchor in his boat, he went downtown to the Plaza and bent over the water fountain to drink. The story goes that when he straightened up he was blind."

Grand-nieces Barbara Usina Jones and Gracie Delany Cothron (who both knew Carl) recall that, thereafter unable to make his living from commercial fishing, he sat in the Plaza in what some called the slave market and knitted mullet nets. His blindness did not take away his innate sense of weather and tide. Although he visited and ate meals with family members in St. Augustine, he continued for many years to live with his dog on a houseboat and successfully navigated his rowboat from the bay front to "home."

I believe that Carl Canova is the model for what Dr. Patricia Griffin (*Mullet on the Beach: The Minorcans in Florida 1768-1788*, p.154) described as, "One of the apocryphal stories told by Minorcan descendants ... of a nineteenth-century Minorcan, stricken blind .., but nevertheless so skilled in sailing wherever he wanted to in St. Augustine waters that he never ran aground." His wry response in the last line of this poem has been passed down, and chuckled over, for generations.

# Home by Dark

"Got to leave my own warm plate
to get that man to the table.
He knows when the breeze turns
Mama's laid out supper.

Carl, why do you sit in the dark?
The tide's past right. Your dog's done gone.
Even I can hear Cathedral bells
beyond your boat, down to Capo's."

    "Looky here, baby girl: Tourists,
    thick as thieves and buying sunshine.
    Bells ain't never told me: Pack up,
    leave jackleg moola in the park.

    Yankee woman took my picture,
    she said. Her money any good?
    Now hold this needle and don't drop that net.
    You know, sister, to me it's always dark."

Photographs of Carl Canova standing on his houseboat c. 1926; and after he became blind, with sunglasses and a cane c. 1940s; with permission of Gracie Delany Cothron

# Uncle Joe's Song

In her cultural study of the first Florida Menorcans, Dr. Patricia Griffin has well described two characteristics that were central to many St. Augustine Menorcans: the importance of religious practices, and the close relationship with the sea and land. Imagine the dilemma of a 1950s Menorcan fisherman entreated to attend an evening Benediction service when the tide was right. In his heart, he could sing his own version of "O Sanctissima." (If you don't know the tune, think Bing Crosby in *The Bells of St. Mary's.*)

# Uncle Joe's Song

Common man's grace
comes from the sea,
lighthouse blessing
dark moon nights.
Feet salt wet,
coquina sand,
net like rosary
in hand,
I am home,
I am home
in God's
good
plan.

Mother current
feeds my hungry lines,
comforts me
with her breaker light.
Strong with tide,
full with moon,
bend the waves
through my knees.
Soft Menorcan,
soft Menorcan
songs
God
sings.

# The Hurricane Lady

In *Minorcans in Florida: Their History and Heritage*, Jane Quinn tells Ysabel Benét's (1835-1915) story of the St. Augustine Hurricane Lady:

> A cargo ship which used to ply its trade between Spain and St. Augustine was endangered one voyage, by a hurricane. The captain and crew prayed for deliverance in these words: "O Hurricane Lady, if this storm passes and we arrive safely in port, we will give your statue to be enshrined permanently in a St. Augustine home." (p.129)

As they did arrive safely in St. Augustine, they gave the statue of Mary from aboard the ship to the Menorcan Rodriquez family. Since this time, c. 1850 or before, the Madonna has been known as the Hurricane Lady.

Mrs. Rodriquez later passed the Hurricane Lady to her godchild, Ysabel Benét. For many years the Hurricane Lady remained with members of the Benét family, and was venerated privately by St. Augustine residents, who often prayed in her presence for protection from hurricanes and storms.

At the death of Mrs. Rene Benét Haas in 1980, the Hurricane Lady was given to Sister St. Charles and the Sisters of St. Joseph. Miss Hazel Crichlow, who lived near the Benéts during her youth and who also was of Menorcan descent, was instrumental in keeping the story of the Hurricane Lady alive and in helping with the restoration of the Hurricane Lady and her garments.

Since 2003 the Hurricane Lady has been enshrined in the Father Miguel O'Reilly House Museum operated by the Sisters of St. Joseph.

# Hurricane Lady

We've worked hard here, raised strong children,
met our responsibilities.
When the priest asks, we send workers.
We pray with deeds, not only knees.
We've been blessed here; we have freedom.
We can walk down any street.
Yet clear, hot days still mislead us
before winds rage and rivers meet.

O Maria, O Maria, count us not among the lost.
O Maria, O Maria, pray for us, our sorrows' cost.
Kindly, kindly intercede. Calm the wind that breaks the reed.
O Maria, dark Maria, trusted Hurricane Lady.

We've worked hard here, as have others
who came by choice or force to shore.
Sometimes we've suffered, sometimes prospered.
We take it all to Mary's door.
Once in old days, frightened sailors
entreated her to bring them here.
In the storm, the dark Madonna
smiled on them, made skies come clear.

O Maria, O Maria, count us not among the lost.
O Maria, O Maria, pray for us, our sorrows' cost.
Kindly, kindly intercede. Calm the wind that breaks the reed.
O Maria, dark Maria, trusted Hurricane Lady.

We've worked hard here, lived through fury
that each year breaks apart the coast.
We say the prayer of faithful sailors,
"Hurricane Lady, keep us close."
In procession down St. George Street

35

we speak our heart, invoke her name.
Our Blessed Lady carries us,
in faith, beyond the hurricane.

O Maria, O Maria, count us not among the lost.
O Maria, O Maria, pray for us, our sorrows' cost.
Kindly, kindly intercede. Calm the wind that breaks the reed.
O Maria, dark Maria, trusted Hurricane Lady.

Photograph of the Hurricane Lady c. 1980, with permission of Carol Lopez Bradshaw

# Is There a Wine?: Leon Canova

According to folklorist Helen Cooper Floyd:

> Captain Leon Canova was among the most famous Florida Minorcans who lived in the 20th century. Quite possibly the most infamous....He began his seagoing career with his father when he was seven years old and was master of his own boat by the time he was 16 years old....He acquired many nicknames. "Cocum" came from Bahamian natives during his rum-running days, about which I have no first hand information.

I knew Uncle Leon, and he *was* the "prankster, eccentric, and avid trencherman" that Cooper Floyd described. My grandmother had the "first hand information" that Cooper Floyd did not; she delighted in describing Uncle Leon's pockets bulging with cash after a night of rum-running. Overlooked in all the colorful descriptions of his life are the small kindnesses he provided to family members.

# Is There A Wine?

*Captain Leon Canova was among the most famous Florida Minorcans who lived in the 20<sup>th</sup> century. Quite possibly the most infamous....He acquired many nicknames. "Cocum" came from Bahamian natives during his rum-running days, about which I have no first hand information.–* Folklorist Helen Cooper Floyd

For *purr-low*? They ain't no wine,
'less you count pot liquor
or a little 'shine Bubba rigged
before he lit out
and left them babies to feed.
They ain't no wine,
just them little mouths
like birds set 'round a table
with a skimpy pot of chicken neck
or butter bean *purr-low*.

For *purr-low*? They ain't no wine.
They ain't none of Leon's rum.
You remember old Cocum?
Cape May to them islands he run
and laughed with them shrimpers
'bout the 'coconut' trade.
They ain't no wine. Never was no wine.
Just now and then a bucket of shrimp
Leon left on the stoop
to feed his nephew's children.

purr-low: pilau

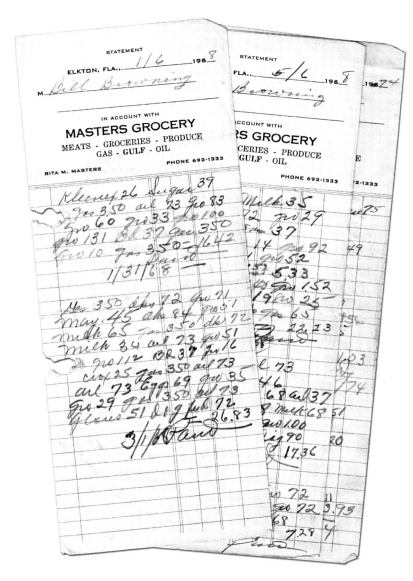

Photograph of billing tabs from Miss Rita Masters' Grocery Store, author's collection

# Miss Rita Masters' Grocery

Miss Rita Masters owned the other country store in Elkton. The strong Menorcan lady held the farming hub together, let folks run a tab, and ran an orderly establishment. Before we had 911 to dial, we had Miss Rita.

During harvest season she kept long hours for potato graders who worked into the night. All of Elkton came alive for a few months as graders readied stock for shipping in chilled rail cars to northern chipping plants.

She had a steady stream of customers. Community college students passing through on their way to Palatka found some form of breakfast or snack there. Her low-slung soft drink coolers were polished daily by the posteriors of the farming area's leaders. In winter, her pot-bellied stove gave children waiting for the school bus the unique experience of freezing on one side and roasting alive on the other.

When she died, she took the community with her.

# Miss Rita Masters' Grocery

Miss Rita,
kin I pump me two dolla
and you put me in your book
'til Friday?

Miss Rita,
Mama says you got any more of that
rat cheese on the chop block
'cause she's gonna make a big macaroni.

Miss Rita,
tonight we gonna grade
'til the cows come home.
You ain't goin' to shut up at six?

Miss Rita,
call Sammy! Call the am-bu-lance!
They's a car in the ditch
and they still breathin'!

Miss Rita,
we surely miss you jokin' us
by the soda cooler in Elkton,
but we proud
God love you so fierce
He took you quick.


rat cheese: rounds or bars of Cheddar cheese

# Nana Explains Life and Death

Catherine Pellicer (1904-1985) belonged to the Canova family group described in this *St. Augustine Record* article on April 21, 2002:

> More than 100 members of Minorcan clan attend reunion

Over 100 Minorcan descendants of the nine children of Alexander Canova and Helen (Ella) Josephine Pacetti (c. 1850) attended the first annual Canova/Pacetti/Delany/Usina reunion April 13th at Glenda and Robert Frawley's hunting grounds near Faver-Dykes State Park. Five generations were present at this first of what is planned to be an annual event. Among the memories shared was a reading titled "My Minorcan Grandfather" by author and story-teller Jeanine Auth.

The relative who traveled farthest to attend, from Cape May, N.J., was John Vonna, grandson of Leon Canova. Leon Canova was known from Cape May to Bimini as a commercial fishing captain and for his prohibition-era "help for thirsty people."

Other Canova siblings that local residents may remember are Grace Canova McBride, who with her husband operated a restaurant at the former site of Maronel Shoe Shop and current site of Pizza Alley on St. George Street; and Blanche Canova Cerveau, whose historic Cerveau home is still in use as a business site on Cuna Street. Local Canova-Pacetti descendants have been or are employed in commercial fishing, banking, business, and education.

# Nana Explains Life and Death

A thousand wisdoms scatter
when an old person dies.
Some we never recover.
When I met Nana walking
on St. George Street in my dream,
she had recovered it all.
At first I was like a hollow bowl
and then I just filled up,
is how she explained death.

Catherine Pellicer
was a butterfly on this street,
one flight path ahead of sorrow.
Practitioner of the geographic cure
and delight of the moving drays,
she was always fine as kine.
In life she spun laughter
from common things, dark nights,
distant memories recast.

*Oooh, no, not a drop of water*
*after midnight, them convent girls*
*would fall out on the way to Mass.*
*I didn't care nothing about school.*
*I'd hop that trolley to the lighthouse*
*and go crab with my Grandmama.*
*When Leon came back late at night,*
*He'd pile rum-running money*
*all over his and Molly's bed.*

*Do you remember how my Daddy*
*rode Margie's old tricycle drunk*
*the night before she married?*
*How my grandfather would stand*

45

*in his nightshirt on the balcony*
*and call me down this very street?*
*How Blanche and Grace said darl-ling*
*and e-nun-ci-a-ted*
*like good Me-nor-cans?*

*Boy, howdy, Harry and I could dance.*
*Once he stayed out all night,*
*came home with his clothes torn.*
*But I didn't say a word.*
*And he never did it again.*
*I could follow Fred just like a man,*
*hold that gun over my head*
*when we waded through the swamp.*
*Those were some happy times.*

She left the Depression with
stories of a goat on the table,
glad to eat a bate of anything.
She rose in middle-night
to butter and savor saltines
Her deepest pain we couldn't mend.
Late afternoon was the hardest
when I lost Harry, and then Fred.
*I kept looking at the screen door.*

She fed our hearts in the best ways.
You had to laugh when she called
your old boyfriend's new girl
as plain as a mud fence.
I didn't want the street to end.
What happens with three ghost husbands?
She hooted and fixed me with eyes
free now from Coke bottle glasses.
*Like after marriage, some day you'll know.*

kine: pronounced kīn (rhymes with fine); Middle English plural of cow; used in a Southern phrase to indicate contentment

bate: pronounced bait; a considerable amount of something, usually food; definitely not a bite

Photograph of Catherine Urbana Pellicer with her parents, Elmanuel Aguiar Pellicer and Bertha Canova Pellicer c. 1910, with permission of Donna Campbell Swan

# For the Children: Pilau and Datil

*Per-loo? Pee-low? Paella?* These are some of the questions heard when pilau is presented. The tomato-roux-based rice dish is pronounced pearl-low. And, yes, it is akin to pilaf with seafood or meat, or a one-meat or one-seafood paella, minus the saffron. But, how does the "r" get in the first syllable? It is a Menorcan-American mystery.

Then there are datil peppers. Datil is pronounced dat (like who-dat)-till.

Datil peppers and pilau go together like popcorn and movies. Their correct pronunciation by newcomers is always a source of amazement to natives.

# For the Children: Pilau and Datil

Some for countra
and some for thee,
whose grandparents came
across the sea.

Knit.
Purl.
Menorcan
twirl.
That's how
we learn
pilau.
Boat.
Row.
Mullet net
throw.
That's how
we learn
pilau.

Purr.
Pearl.
Snake-belly
low.
That's how
we learn
pilau.

That
cat
countra made
fat.
That's how
we learn

datil.

Pie
still
warming the
sill.
That's how
we learn
datil.

Scat,
Bill,
over the
hill.
That's how
we learn
datil.

Some for countra
and some for thee,
pilau and datil
Menorcan be.

countra: pronounced coon´trah; a St. Augustine Menorcan word meaning "a
little extra is given," like a baker's dozen or a lagniappe

# You Want Mullet?

The cry "Mullet on the beach!" was a marching order that usually came in June. It meant that a dark, wide, trembling streak of a school of mullet was moving like a demonic oil slick off-shore. If any man had thoughts of fresh fried mullet or enough smoked mullet for family and neighborhood, this was the time to hit the beach.

Two old stories exist that show the potency of this phrase. In the first, a local baseball game being played at Francis Field was interrupted by a man shouting "Mullet on the beach!" The game immediately ended with players scrambling to go home for their mullet nets. In the second, the Cathedral door was opened and the phrase was shouted during a Mass. This, of course, left mostly women, and children firmly clasped by women, to finish the service.

# You Want Mullet?

*They are running. Mother of God, they are running!*

You want mullet?
Get yourself down there
in your skeeter
and throw that net
until your shoulders grind your spine.

Or is it dreams that bump
under darting water,
singing like orca
while you sleepwalk highways
and dead offices?

Who watches the long ripple for you
and runs crying
"Mullet!"
"Mullet on the beach!"
and shakes you open
to the one time
you can cast anywhere
but over your brother's head
and be fed?

skeeter: a stripped-down vehicle, sometimes with wooden body replacements,
used to cruise the beach or to haul people to fish on the beach

# Cultural Myth and Cultural Drift:

*Datil Peppers and Fromajardis*

There is a great St. Augustine myth that datil peppers arrived in St. Augustine with Menorcan settlers. This is written in many places describing St. Augustine foods, even in a 1950s local hospital auxiliary recipe booklet. So you can imagine the author's surprise in a 2004 visit to Menorca when no Menorcans encountered had a clue about this incredibly hot pepper. There is no mention of them in the Menorcan History Museum in Menorca's capital city, Mahon. And in Castilian and Catalan dialects of Spanish, the word datil actually means date, not even a close relation to a hot pepper.

In three more visits to Menorca since 2004, the author has not found datil pepper plants growing there. Unless they have recently arrived as transplants from St. Augustine, it seems that they are a New World variety of pepper.

A second part of the myth is that datil peppers will only grow in the St. Augustine area. The author's brother-in-law grew fine crops of them in Alabama. A quick internet search showed them being grown as far away as Illinois.

How, then, did this belief arise in Menorcan and non-Menorcan St. Augustine residents? The only theory offered here is that St. Augustine Menorcans have been using the pepper a long, long time with delightful results. It is so associated with this cultural group that a logical, but now not plausible, supposition would be that they brought the pepper with them.

When sharing this myth-busting information at a recent Menorcan Festival, the author was told she'd made a participant's grandmother twirl in her grave. Please don't shoot the messenger. Instead, see Dr. Daniel Cantliffe's enlightening work on this pepper's migration from South America.

And then there's cultural drift for another Menorcan food. Fromajardis are a Menorcan cheese pastry usually served at Easter.

On the same 2004 trip to Menorca mentioned above, fromajardis were served at dinner in Dr. Victoriano Seoane-Pascucci's home.

Dr. Seoane-Pascucci and his wife Maria had a good laugh at our faces when we realized that the fromajardis *were* dinner, and not dessert. That was the second thing we noticed, after realizing that they didn't look like the St. Augustine round or crescent pastry, that there was no small cross scored on top that some St. Augustine Menorcan cooks used to expose the cheese filling. He explained that the reason they held beef, pork, fish, or fruit, instead of cheese, was that the British had controlled the island for so long that the traditional fromajardis had morphed into something like beef pasties.

Fromajardis were brought from Menorca, but Menorcan-Americans may be the only ones using the original recipe!

Photograph of datil peppers 2008, with permission of Dr. Daniel Cantliffe

# The St. Augustine Menorcan Litmus Test

Did we bring datil peppers from Menorca?
Did we bring datil peppers from New Smyrna?
Did we find datil peppers locked in the Fort?
None of this matters, unless you are Menorcan.

The St. Augustine Menorcan litmus test
begins with the green and orange beauties
that you grow in five-gallon pickle buckets,
unless your parents or in-laws give you a handful.

Put gloves on your Mediterranean hands,
for you are about to slice hell-fire, Cousin,
from a two-inch pepper guaranteed
to burn you up alive with those innocent white seeds.

Throw those seeds away and chop up that pepper!
Sprinkle that flaming dice on some fine pilau;
and if you don't have pilau, use beans and rice.
And if you don't have beans and rice, are you Menorcan?

But I digress. Now take a bite. Eat it all.
Can you still talk? Do you want the garden hose?
If you like what you ate, if you would eat more,
we will then call you a g-o-o-o-d Menorcan.

# III  Cattle-Whip Crackers

# We Ain't Scufflin'

What exactly is a country kitchen? In this case, it refers to Fred and Catherine Pellicer Klipstine's large Cracker-Menorcan kitchen added to a modest home on a very small farm. Silver Queen corn, sweet potatoes, and datil peppers rotated by season in the plot by their home. But their crops didn't all go just from field to customers. Datil peppers were also made into relish that simmered for six hours a batch. And datil peppers were put up in vinegar to season greens and any other dish that cried out for liquid fire. Counter and storage space were needed to prepare and house these incendiary products.

Catherine also had a double oven. She sold fruit cakes and pound cakes, turning the kitchen into a bakery production line. There was space, space, and more space in her country kitchen that ran across the entire back of the home.

Fred and Catherine weren't scuffling. They were hustling to make a living off of their small homestead. The country kitchen provided space for cooking, processing, and storing their farm wares.

There was even enough space to put a double bed in the corner of the kitchen. It came in handy when a grown child temporarily needed a place to land.

# We Ain't Scufflin'

Son,
we got you a bed
in the kitchen.

Bed
in the kitchen.

No.
No, it prob'ly ain't
like coming home
from the war.
'Member you wanting
to jump
right offen
that train
into the salt marsh?
Mmm-hmmm.

Son,
*you know*
we got a country kitchen.
And we ain't stickin' you
in the pantry.
That bed's
going to butt up
right next
to the breezeway screen door.
I'll tell that old heifer 'cross the way
you kin do something for her boy.
He come to be a big boss.

Now,
WE AIN'T SCUFFLIN'.
I been sellin' bushels

of Silver Queen
and we done got
two month of tractor work.
Winn Dixie
even took
the datil peppers.
We going to get along
just fine
as kine.

# Widger and Waukie and Me

Everyone who worked on a farm wasn't fortunate enough to own it. Seasonal workers, migrant workers, labor crews, temporary hands who lived in the community – there were many situations and names for those working the land. For those who would move on after crops were harvested, living conditions were never ideal. After World War II, some labor crews lived in a barracks near Hasting that was previously used to house prisoners of war.

It was a hard life. But, sometimes, the spark of human kindness shone through.

# Widger and Waukie and Me

Widger and Waukie and me went to the store
each week. Waukie said Widge never knew
a kind hand, so we had to neighbor-like
smooth his hard edges. Thas how we come to
getting him oxygen air and tubes in June.

Used to be, Widge kept boss-man away
from me when we finished the field.
Now he had to sit in Waukie's rocker
a long time after he drug over to eat.
But still his marbles was all right there.

He was almost growed, yet come August
Waukie tucked him in just like me.
Sundays she'd stare down his old deddy
while she washed Widge before preacher came.
Widge got shorted young, but we kept him
good as we could. Like we keep his grave.

# Hurricane

Old-time St. Augustinians remember when one could ride south from St. Augustine Beach and see miles of dunes punctuated by the occasional beach house or small beach motel. Some viewed these dunes as they rode the Marineland bus sent to downtown St. Augustine to pick up employees. In the old days, not that many people lived at the beaches.

Common knowledge among most common folk was that beach houses shouldn't have too much heart or valuables put into them. Everyone remembered when a nor'easter or hurricane had joined the San Sebastian River to the bay front, flooding the city. Charley Sanchez described walking waist-high in water down Cordova Street to his home near old Flagler Hospital in the 1940s. And residents who were able to ride to Vilano Beach after Hurricane Dora in 1964 were horrified to see slab after slab where homes *had* been on the ocean side of A1A.

Yet, what do we do when a major storm or hurricane approaches? We are the maniacs who go to the bay front, pier, or beach entrance to be sandblasted by wind and anointed by wild, frothy sea spray. We usually do leave candles, batteries, the occasional generator, and lots of comfort food at home. And we know when to return there.

# Hurricane

Ululations
to the builders
of condos on dunes,
to sand barons
who swear
that the ocean
never raves
beyond high tide.
Yet here we are,
witnesses called
to drive wrong-way
on a banshee beach,
to flap like crazed
hurricane angels,
stung to life
by lasers of sand.

We knew how
a beach house
*should be* raggedy.
We knew how
to love the wild mother
from a *distance*,
with tins of food
and pots of water,
pilau and pound cake
cooked to keep us
when the power went.
And we knew
how to leave
in the last crack
of drivable wind.

# The Casino

Richard Parks was a talented musician who later became a St. Johns County Commissioner. Beginning in 1926, locals and tourists boarded a horse-drawn trolley or came by launch to hear his band at the Casino on Vilano Beach. After 1931, they were able to travel to the Casino on a less-demanding paved highway. The Casino lasted until 1937, done in by storms that battered St. Augustine's coast.

The owner of the Casino struggled to prevent its collapse. Wooden, concrete, and steel bulkheads were erected to keep back the waves that moved further in with each nor'easter. When interviewed by Jackie Feagin concerning her memories of this time, Mary B. Usina said, "That old inlet was just determined to pull that sand away and it did."

# The Casino

Dick Parks played *By the Beautiful Sea*,
pelting night with the musical score.
Our grandparents danced on boards over dunes
swaying now on the ocean floor.

Sandbagging, dredging, and rip-rap hedging
must make God and the Goddess laugh here.
Old native, new builder, which one was heard
by an Army Corps engineer?

Money has won and memory has lost,
where people build high on beach sand.
But storms will still shift the Eastern coast
after we've joined Dick Parks and his band.

The ruin of Florida is not yet complete.
Can she be forgiving if cities meet
in dunes become concrete, marsh paved dry?

She waits for Atlantis in the hurricane eye.

# Thelma Padgett's Home

*Across From the Methodist Church*

Mrs. Thelma Padgett allowed her home to become a Bride's House on wedding days. Her care helped make hopeful magic that floated across the street to the Methodist Church.

# Thelma Padgett's Home

*Across From the Methodist Church*

Come the young women
to enter the Bride's House,
to marry in Hastings.
Come the young women
with hope in their hair,
with life in their hands.

Come the young women
to enter the Bride's House,
led sometimes by fathers
who pocket their fear.
Come the young women
as mothers have planned.

Come the young women
to enter the Bride's House,
to crimp the last ribbon,
to plait the new path.
Come the young women
to sever, then bind.

Come the young women
to enter the Bride's House,
to pass through the heart
of Thelma, bridge keeper.
Come the young women
full awake, so they think.

# Paul Victor, December 1941

News of the Pearl Harbor bombing came late in the afternoon to St. Augustine residents. Some wondered if their country relatives had a radio on that picked up the devastating news. Even if they had telephones, it was not the kind of news to be delivered on a party line. So they piled into their cars and went west toward Bakersville, Spuds, Molasses Junction to be the bearers of what no one wants to bring.

# Paul Victor, December 1941

Sometimes Paul Victor, Senior,
scared the tar from young bucks.
But late that Sunday afternoon he wept,
wept man tears we'd never seen in a country store.
"You boys go on home," he said,
pouring "boys" like wine on our heads.
"You boys tend to your families.
Get on home now."

Next Sunday before Mass
he rang the bell like always.
Then, "Listen here, Bubba," he told Daddy,
"I'll keep the quietus on them boys upstairs."
And upstairs P.V. drove the herd of us,
upstairs where he'd reigned like a stag
over every yowling christening
and each new stone-faced widda.

We teared up pretty bad when
the priest sang prayers for Paul Victor, Junior,
jaw muscles working on a world gone to shards.
Lord, how the old stoic led us knuckleheads
to genuflect, I will never know.
Winding down the bell tower past him,
he cuffed us all with a gentle man's palm,
the only time he ever touched us.

I loved that old man.

# IV  And After

# Vernon and Moses Tell It at the Depot

St. Augustine was still a small Southern town in the 1940s. Hack, or carriage, drivers still waited at the train depot to pick up tourists. Sometimes, instead of carrying a traveler from the North to a hotel, a hack driver would be hired by a local man to pick up a returning family member and carry them home through the streets of St. Augustine.

Photograph of Florida East Coast Railway Depot with hacks waiting to carry passengers to local hotels c. 1910, with permission of State Archives of Florida

# Vernon and Moses Tell It at the Depot

Vernon:  "Tell it, man: pan-fish and lowdown. Tell it
before Sunshine pull in and nags haul out.
Tell it. Moses, I be 'round tonight
if sheephead in your ice box.

Tell it. Before Yankee man pile off,
talk like fake kin: 'Oh, Sonny. Uncle? Boy!'
Tell it. Tell it before brother porter
jump down, jive nice like they all family."

Moses:  "I come for Mister Challey's daughter.
He ain't got no rippy, no store-time off.
They white, but act like they
scufflin' like the rest of us.

Look like they doin' life and death.
She nursin' at the Flagler,
he fixin' some widda-lady tom-cat,
then sellin' you a headstone on the side.

He pay fair enough. I ain't waste no
thirty Yankee minutes haulin' a gal
for some Cracker in a sheet.
I got life and death goin', too."

Vernon: "Law', you be haulin' the whole town
if some Cracker-sheet say 'Haul!'
Tell it. Speak the truth before God."

Moses:  "I'd be haulin'. *My* children. The other way."

rippy:   a cut-down Model A or T with a truck bed on the back; used for hauling
fixin':   neutering

# Periwinkle Stew

*Donax variabilis* are the small clams that make up the coquina rock still seen in St. Augustine architecture. They are known locally as periwinkles. St. Augustine's waters have always provided food for the table and extra income. This was especially helpful before passage of the Civil Rights Act, when African Americans were hired mostly for menial jobs and were often paid less than their white counterparts in the South.

Johnny Mae Brown (1905-2000) moved to Elkton as a young woman and worked at different times as a housekeeper for the Sanchez and Ivey families. One of the many things that she explained to me was how to make periwinkle stew. Another was that good pilau must be cooked early and allowed to sit and wait. After the seasonings "married," pilau could be gently reheated. It would taste even better the next day.

# Periiwinkle Stew

## I

On rising tide they scoot,
geysers bursting along
in cloudy salt water
above washboard bottom.
On low tide they dive,
a covey of bullets
like baby torpedoes
that wiggle in the sand.
Mostly, they are dug-in
just below water's edge,
growing tighter in the shell,
feeling the moon and sun.

## II

"Honey, we'd barely scrape the surface
and get 'em by the bucketful.
Lord, they boiled in big wash pots.
They didn't need no salt!
Now the moon would tell you
when to go, but we liked
to go toward the weekend.
You know, those rich people
in the hotels really loved
that meat and broth
and they were willin' to pay
for that periwinkle stew."

# Sister Mary Trinita

In 1866, eight volunteers from the Sisters of St. Joseph in Le Puy, France, came to St. Augustine at the invitation of Bishop Augustin Verot.

St. Agnes School was one of the schools where the Sisters of St. Joseph taught. Through the 1950s, it was located in what was known as North City in St. Augustine. Garnett's orange grove, a vestige of the North Florida citrus industry that remained after the freeze line moved south, was across the street from the school and was regularly invaded by St. Agnes students. The old wooden school building has been replaced by a concrete block one that now houses an early childhood education center.

# Sister Mary Trinita

*God did not say, go to the east to find wisdom, sail to
the west to find justice: there where you seek, you shall
find, for to Him who is everywhere present, one comes
by love and not by sail.* – St. Augustine

She came to us
by love and sail.
We thought her
born like Venus,
fully-formed,
until March-mail
from home
brought shamrocks.
Their mystery
rested emerald
in a black channel
of habit, bound
in the starched white square
that neatened
the unknowing poor.

(It was a sensible square,
known to catch
a drop of salt
from those of us
overwhelmed
by the saints.)

A deeper mystery
was the woman
who asked,
"Would you like to see
some *real* shamrocks?"
She held them

gently as
my heart still holds
her eyes, her smile,
touched
through time
that she
over water moved
to confess
unseen ties.

Photographs of wooden St. Agnes School and the St. Agnes Church, and of Sisters Mary Trinita, Alice Joseph, and Mary Edwina c. 1959-60, author's collection, with permission of Sisters of St. Joseph, St. Augustine

# Old City Divorce

Every Catholic school child of the Fifties knew that divorced people went to hell. Particularly the divorced women of St. Augustine. On their way, divorced women had the opportunity to prepare for damnation by working in luncheonettes and tourist attractions, where women who "had" to earn a living sometimes also earned contempt. Guiding tourists or serving pilau, barbecue, or fried shrimp to locals were some ways to get by.

# Old City Divorce

*In those days respectable women didn't work as wait-*
*resses.* —Cecil Pacetti

Unchurched women
could stomp tips and rent
and the power bill
from any mean floor.

For this, the Spanish God
gave St. Augustine women
an audience of tourists
and the still-joined.

Perditious hands passed
sulphur water
to strangers gouging romance
from mantillas.

The damned served dreams
gutted and fried
to women wearing gold bands,
women home in the afternoon.

A thousand Aves away
from absolution, the children
of these good, doomed mothers
think they hate the priest.

Come.
Drink my water.
See my heart
at the bottom of the cup.

# Easter Frost

Before a shopping mall opened in St. Augustine in the 1970s, families who could afford to travel to Jacksonville or Orlando to shop, often did. The rest of St. Augustine made do, sewed, redid, or shopped in the local stores on St. George and King Streets.

Prior to the coming of the mall, Christmas and Easter shopping on St. George Street was a street-long family reunion. But, there was still a pecking order for spring sweaters and Easter hats that were worn through the 1960s, even if they came from the dime store.

# Easter Frost

We wore white sweaters
for Easter frost. We
sniggered at Margie's
scruffy brown jacket,
her legs without hose,
her bobby pins and
folded tissues on
burnt Easter-permed hair.
Ammonia made our
hair stink, too, but *we*
wore white sweaters and
dippy Woolworth hats
brought home by mothers
worn-out by fits and
tantrums we threw in
shops where they knew us.
We wore white sweaters,
and our hearts believed
polyester hid
the shiny, cruel knives
we righteously carried
to church and back.

# Saint October

Imagine the view of St. Augustine from the Mill Top, a tavern that sits above a grist mill replica in the Spanish Quarter. At the right time of day, one can ponder both the Castillo de San Marcos and the Usina family sightseeing ship Victory making its tour of the bay. From this vantage, October in St. Augustine is surely a candidate for sainthood.

# Saint October

I worship Saint October
from a Mill Top pew.
The wayward,
wishful drinking,
cannot see
turret candles
or falling morning incense
strewn
as Fort green dew.

Sons and daughters
of Agustin,
they must drink
all the decadence,
waste the empty beach,
let the golden
light of air
fall beyond their reach
before the miracle of
temperature
bends their knees.

Saint October
anoints them
anyway,
heals with a sky
of periwinkle
and shrimp
above Victory in the bay,
and makes
the inadvertent soiree
on holy turquoise
water
a pilgrimage.

# Time on the Bridge

At the top of the Exchange Bank a time/temperature display was visible to those crossing the Bridge of Lions into the downtown plaza area. The City of St. Augustine had the display removed when the building changed hands in 1986 because it no longer met the sign ordinance. The locals thought that strange. After blinking for almost forty years, it was almost a national monument.

Photograph of the Exchange Bank that includes its time/temperature display c. 1960, with permission of the St. Augustine Historical Society

# Time on the Bridge

The Exchange Bank broke the sky
by degrees. Weekend nights we
on the bridge counted time into air
from a six story warning of
mama's eye and daddy's voice.

Fords and Chevys gunned summer's
roller coaster drop from the bay.
"That can't be right!" we screamed.
We moaned. We prayed for green at the
end of our probable last ride.

But going over, oh, going
over. Look back, look back to
see how long we're free: until
76 degrees turns to midnight.
It was always later than we thought.

# 1966 Reunion

At least two versions exist of how Porpoise Point was named. One is that dolphins or porpoise were trapped in a slough in the area. The other is that Marineland trainers closed an area off of what became known as Porpoise Point to pen wild dolphins before moving them to the marine attraction. These events being quite before my time, and being forcefully told both views by believers, I can validate neither.

Before the housing explosion at St. Augustine's beaches, however, Porpoise Point was a beach destination for fishermen and families by day, and sometimes before a secluded place for teenaged beer parties by night. A St. Augustine story is that a male teen or teens escaped being collared at one of these parties by swimming across to St. Augustine proper.

A local self-deprecation was that St. Augustine was twenty years behind the customs and fashions of the North. As evidenced by the Porpoise Point beer parties, by the 1960s, things were catching up.

Bras, however, weren't being burned in the Plaza by the mid-Sixties. But the Civil Rights Movement had a defining moment of ground zero there. Marriages still occurred shortly after high school graduation and precluded college for the newlyweds. But the cultural group of Floridanos, Menorcans, and Cattle-Whip Crackers was not as homogenized as twenty years earlier. First family members were beginning to attend college, even "girls."

The Vietnam War was also a forceful influence for acculturation. As was happening around the country, some went to college to avoid the draft. And some went to war.

# 1966 Reunion

Remember who swam
from Porpoise Point
when the cops showed up?
Remember they got him
anyway, on the city side?
God, the screechin' girls.
Even Jack had a melt-down
when his mom popped him.
Damn lucky we boneheads
had graduated two hours ago.

Then, somehow, we all rode away.
Mamas sobbed, but glad daddies
gave up the in-crowd to dorms
where trees had seasons.
Bewildered new husbands
blistered the road to Daytona
for weekend honeymoons.
And we bad boys just acted tough
on Uncle Sam's leased jet
to an endless summer.

# Into the Neighborhood

One summer dark, porch-sitting night when I was about ten, I asked my Grandfather Sanchez if relatives from the Old Country had ever visited us.

"Yes," he said.

Wow. I had found a gold mine. "Where were they from?" I asked.

"I think they called it Quinca, or something like that," he replied.

"What were they like?" I continued.

"Well," he reflected, "we didn't have much to do with them."

Then the conversation turned to daily life, gossip from the customers to whom he sold Fuller Brush products, and what went on in Mass last Sunday.

Half-a-dozen years later, I walked hand-in-hand with my grandfather through the plaza toward my first job, which he had arranged. Mr. and Mrs. Brunson owned the Battle House Restaurant on Cathedral Place, and they needed a summer waitress. They were local, kind, and sure to keep my sixteen-year-old self in line just like family.

# Into the Neighborhood

Puente's map was lost on us.
We lived in a new mother country,
though we still kept to family ways.
We no longer waited on tides,
seasons, horseback couriers.
Instead, we peered down driveways
or walked to a newspaper box,
and sat on afternoon porches
or in after-supper-dishes kitchens
to read the St. Augustine Record.

We called our neighborhoods
Pablo Beach, Vilano Beach,
North City, Rabbit Hill,
Santa Rosa, New Augustine,
West Augustine, Lincolnville,
Downtown, Davis Shores,
and out to running country,
Tocoi, Molasses Junction,
Elkton, Moccasin Branch,
Armstrong, Hastings.

But their real names were
Got-to-be-near-business,
Must-live-near-Mama-and-Daddy,
Can't-be-cooped-up,
Have-to-be-near-the-water,
Wouldn't-live-anywhere-else,
Can't-afford-any-better,
Love-my-woods,
Like-to-look-over-fields,
and Not-fooling-anyone.

The Fuller Brush man explained

this comfortable geography
to his grandchildren,
then charted territories
that led every other Friday
to the off-world of Crescent Beach,
A1A's dunes and beaches,
and long swoops of pelicans.
He brought home reports
that people lived at Marineland.

His eldest grandchild
burned to make her way.
So hand-in-hand they walked
into the neighborhood
across from the Plaza.
He knew the old couple there
commanded a respectable café,
and, hired only local help.
They would not let her
travel on too far.

Puente: pronounced Pwayn-tay; Spanish cartographer of early Spanish colo-
nial St. Augustine

# Johnny Mae Kept Us,
# But Plessy Had Us All

Before 1964, much of Johnny Mae Brown's life was ruled by the 1896 Supreme Court case Plessy versus Ferguson. Plessy allowed separate rail cars for black and white passengers, and was used to justify the alleged "separate but equal" system of segregation.

In the late 1950s Ms. Brown's daughter died. Ms. Brown raised her daughter's five children while working as a housekeeper and tending Sanchez grandchildren.

As a child, I didn't understand why Ms. Brown said, "We can eat our hot dog in the park." It was the 1960s and we stood in my grandparents' kitchen. And I didn't know until her wake that she thought the irony of being moved from the black rail car to the white rail car to care for my very fussy young cousin was a hoot.

# Johnny Mae Kept Us,
# But Plessy Had Us All

STATES MAY REQUIRE SEPARATE
CARS FOR THE TWO RACES

Washington, D.C., May 18 – The supreme court (sic) today, in an opinion read by Justice Brown, sustained the constitutionality of the law of Louisiana requiring the railroads of that state to provide separate cars for white and colored passengers.

The [Plessy v. Ferguson] opinion states that by analogy to the laws of congress and of many of the states requiring the establishment of separate schools for children of the two races, and other similar laws, the statute in question was within the competency of the Louisiana legislature exercising police power of the state.

Mr. Justice Harlan announced a very vigorous dissent, saying that he saw nothing but mischief in all such laws. In his view of the case no power of the land had the right to regulate the enjoyment of civil rights on the basis of race. – *Florida Times-Union*, May 19, 1896

One blue-cold day in my babygirl-hood,
in a house teased by a kerosene heater,
she bathed me, swaddled me,
dried and warmed me by a hearth
she'd had time and care enough to lay.

This memory made her blood-children sad.

Before Dr. King lit our streets, before
a snapped-nerve summer of guarded dime stores,
before lunch counters stomped away aghast
that Cook's spoiled child refused to eat outside,
she spoke through my tattling lips.

She spoke through my tattling lips
before my learning overrode love, before
I recognized a mama bird dragging
a wise wing far, far away from her nest.
"We can eat our hot dog on the park bench," she said.

This memory made me sad.

Sometimes funeral truth speaks what we need.
My young cousin B.G. once raised such sand
wanting her, that the train boss lost his mind.
So she strolled past Plessy to the white people's car.
"How she laughed telling it," her granddaughter said.

We children laughed, too, at the wake.

# Three Years Later: Marineland, Summer 1967

After Dr. King's visit to St. Augustine, after marches and dem-onstrations, after Klan intimidation and violence, the Civil Rights Act was signed July 2, 1964. Then, on June 12, 1967, the Supreme Court overturned state miscegenation laws that prohibited blacks and whites from marrying.

As the South was, St. Augustine was. St. Augustine began to make the slow outward transition to an integrated community.

In the summer of 1967, black and white young people worked together in the tourist trade. Questions could still be asked that, in the past, had resulted in lynching. Now, answers varied. Some still feared reprisals. Others bravely opened doors.

# Three Years Later: Marineland, Summer 1967

*If I came to a dance at your high school, would you dance with me?*

Pooled dolphins danced the hours
and we fed the beat of shows in shifts.
You cooked, I served. Tourists thrummed on,
answering the trainer's snap, unaware
that to our east the hidden service path
led to free dolphins rising in open water.

Would I dance with you? Would I touch your skin?
Your seventeen had courage more than mine.
My hand in yours could still burn down our homes.
We could be-bop a noose around your neck.
I feared white whiteness and my own pale arms.
Even free dolphins can hesitate in the air.

I didn't break the surface
of my holding pond for breath:
*I have a boyfriend...I have a boyfriend*
*and, if I dance, I only dance with him.*
Let me go. Let me swim in small, safe pools.
For food, friends, old age, let me rise through hoops.

*But, if you didn't have a boyfriend?*
your brown eyes asked. East of morning,
a hundred yards and a life away,
the ocean gave up arcs of light,
reflecting dolphins. We watched them bow,
rising in open water to inhale, to dance.

# Summer Dark Porch-Sitting Nights

After the mid-1960s, there didn't seem to be as many fruit or fish peddlers with bicycles or carts. Students may have still bowed their heads and crossed themselves as they walked in front of the Cathedral, but they stopped actually genuflecting in front of the Cathedral door. No more tissues on forgetful heads at Mass. Some college students who had been raised in prejudice came home to blow off the roof at Thanksgiving. The 400th anniversary of St. Augustine's founding had changed buildings in our downtown.

We may have still been sitting in rockers on porches, if air-conditioning had not yet made its way to our home, but our days and nights were forever changed. We were hurtling toward a real man on the moon.

turtle-eggin': the no-longer legal practice of removing eggs from a sea turtle's nest, carried out at night after the sea turtle has deposited the eggs in a shore nest and returned to the ocean. When this was legal, mindful St. Augustinians removed only a portion of the eggs. A boiled turtle egg never completely solidifies.

# Summer Dark Porch-Sitting Nights

Summer dark porch-sitting nights
led me to believe I'd live forever
here. Even Nana,
without a silhouette in her rocker,
sounded eternal.
Before we knew who we were,
turtle eggin' had joined
us to the ocean, and the dunes
had given us to each other.

When we thought to look,
it was gone. New neighbors
confabulate a shore line
brought only by the next storm.
They never climbed for tangerines,
never winced from kumquats.
The mullet man never sang
fish or fruit on their street.

Tradition pitty-patted out of town
without even a good-bye drink
at Shrimp Haven. Forget
someone's Mama's guava jelly.
Saturday night Mass will do you.
The Sisters who sweatered
bare-armed girls from sin
are dancing hula hoops
over what now prays in the Cathedral.

And the rest of us have also juked.

# How Can I Move Here?

Emmett Fritz came to St. Augustine in 1950, and for over forty years was St. Augustine's unofficial artist-in-residence on St. George Street. After his death in 1995, *St. Augustine Record* Associate Editor Margo Pope wrote:

> Fritz' paintings stand out in my mind with those of the Flagler Era artists – DeCrano, Shapleigh, Drown. Theirs recorded the spirit of an age long past. His detail the great changes in our historic places over 45 years. At *The Record,* we have a classic Fritz: a view of St. George Street with the Cathedral-Basilica of St. Augustine in the center, and a horse and buggy headed north – when the street was still open that way.

# How Can I Move Here?

Many years later they will say,
"I went to the Fort once."

But their skin's memory
carries the unseen
of small morning haze unlocked from the bay,
holding a foot of tension above water
two months past solstice.
And with a collective turning in bed,
hope from the comforter
of St. Augustine
is still tucked
around the traveler
and the traveler's children.

East sun on Ponce bougainvillea
flamed a cerise frisson
up finely veined walls,
exploded buff cream
from under terra cotta roofs,
pierced their eyes like
Mary's heart in the Cathedral.
But they heard
eggs hissing
on the St. George Pharmacy grill.
Their stomachs relaxed
with a sinking
net plop
in the San Sebastian.
When a redeeming crane
carried a jump in their chest
away to the Shrine pond,
they wondered,
"How can I move here?"

Oh, they will say,
"I went to the Fort once."
But somewhere they are walking
on an Emmett Fritz street,
telling time
by the color of water in the bay.

# Vermeer in St. Augustine

The sun has crossed east to west down the King's street in St. Augustine for a long time. But its light did not fall as it does now until tourism, trains, and trade began to spirit away the tree canopy that covered the city. Old old-timers, now gone, laughed telling how they were almost able to cross town branch-to-branch as boys.

Now we have blocks of buildings on King Street, some humble, some majestic, for the west sun to illuminate before it descends past the lighthouse into the ocean. We have seasons of light that pour from Ponce de Leon Boulevard: April ease, July haze, January crystal.

It is the first two weeks of November light, though, that could draw Vermeer's ghost to St. Augustine. Transfiguring light just past the ripe pearl light of October. Rich, yet sheer, warm incandescence before the chill December light that turns the San Sebastian River cobalt.

# Vermeer in St. Augustine

Vermeer in St. Augustine wept
when five p.m. November light
cracked from a boulevard magnum.
"Ohh," he breathed,
then inhaled a trail of arctic shimmer
before it leapt the San Sebastian,
before freezing white minutes percussed
east down the King's street,
texturing mica on railway building totems,
sheeting diamond dust
on a post office block
asleep under back-lit palms
and glints of loquat yellow.

Ivory kindled and sparked from the electric sea,
transfigured the Ponce, Cordova, Alcazar,
crashed in a wave at the Governor's House
and mounted the Episcopalian steeple.
Saints rode breakneck up basilica light.
The long radiance hesitated, gyred,
arced above the plaza,
leaving sepia to mantle the revenants
murmuring under live oaks.
Vermeer left them, shining darkly,
unseeing among unlit alabaster.

Crystal unspooled across the Lions' Bridge.
Champagne rinsed dusk from the air,
illumined the lighthouse, gilded
the afternoon's last beach walk
to night's summoning road,
eternity crashing,
crashing at its side.
He tinged the last clear light pale blue.

Before the flare of a rose wave,
it quivered, transparent again,
and drove blushing into an indigo throat.

At last the hands of Vermeer
told the curve of the earth,
the delirium of its beauty,
the light only here. He wept,
and did not care if he rushed
our play, our death. He saw
this light will not be written,
nor richly brushed,
hiding faces, walls, messengers.
He plaited incandescence,
thick as pearls
across the hollow of a day.

# Epilogue: Pages from a Menorcan Diary

## March 2004

### A St. Ambrose Fair without Pilau

When pilau went away from the St. Ambrose Fair, we were shocked. No tender rice browned with a tomato roux that took an hour to cook down; no marriage of bell peppers and onion, bay leaf, and thyme. Where else would we find our poor man's paella?

It won't be the same, I groused as a city Menorcan. I didn't spend a week chopping and cooking for the first part of humble, magical pilau. I wouldn't be locked in the church hall kitchen the day before the Fair. And I surely would not show up by dawn on Fair Day to complete the noon meal.

It will work out, a country Menorcan told me. We are too old to keep this up and no one else wants the job. Our grandchildren in another city don't even bother to come home for the Fair any more. There's new blood that wants to fry fish dinners. It will work out.

We survived the first Fair without pilau, but not without all parties weighing in on a riceless meal. The Menorcan clam chowder took up the slack for some. We moved under the canopy of live oaks as we had for over a hundred years, catching up, admonishing children, thankful for a spring day that would open the heart of Scrooge.

## March 2005

Pilau returned to the St. Ambrose Fair. Our world was right.

# Bibliography

Bitzer, Sr. Catherine, SSJ. Personal communications. 2014-2015.

Bradshaw, C. L. Telephone interview. 21 June 2005.

Browning, S.S. Personal communications. Friday evenings since 2000.

Bramson, S. 2003. *Speedway to Sunshine: The Story of the Florida East Coast Railway.* 3<sup>rd</sup> ed. Ontario, Canada: Boston Mills Press.

Cantliffe, D. *2008 Proceedings of the Florida State Horticultural Society.* 121: 23-233.

Cathedral Parish Records of St. Augustine, Florida.

Catholic Diocese of St. Augustine Archives.

Cothron, G.D. Personal interview. 16 July 2004.

Crichlow, D. Personal interview. 21 May 2005.

Feagin, J. "Grand Casino Lasted Just Briefly." *St. Augustine Record* 12 July 1985: A1.

Floyd, H. C. 1992. *Mayport Remembered: Along the Waterfront.* Pascagoula, Mississippi: Alpha Printing Co., Inc.

Gannon, M. 2003. *Florida: A Short History.* Gainesville, Florida: University Press of Florida.

Graham, T. 1978. *The Awakening of St. Augustine: The Anderson Family and the Oldest City 1821-1924.* St. Augustine, Florida: St. Augustine Historical Society.

Griffin, P. 1976. Thalassemia: A Case Study of the Minorcans of Florida. Unpublished manuscript at St. Augustine Historical Society.

Griffin, P. 1991. *Mullet on the Beach: The Minorcans of Florida 1768-1788.* Jacksonville, Florida: University Press of Florida.

"History Wreathes Ancient Madonna in St. Augustine." *Florida Catholic* 27 July 1945: 8.

Jones, B. J. 2005. I Can Remember. Unpublished manuscript.

"Lola Sanchez's Ride." *The Confederate Veteran* Aug. 1909: 409-410.

McGoldrick, Sr. Thomas Joseph, SSJ. Personal interview. 13 June 2005.

"More Than 100 Members of Minorcan Clan Attend Reunion." *St. Augustine Record* 21 Apr. 2002: C3.

Pacetti, C. F., Sr. Personal interview. 15 June 1996.

Pascucci, V. S. Personal communications in Menorca 2004-2009.

Pope, M. "City's Better for the Lives of These Three." *St. Augustine Record* 31 Dec.1995.

Powers, R. and F. Personal interview. 22 July 2005.

Quinn, J. 1975. *Minorcans in Florida: Their History and Heritage.* St. Augustine, Florida: Mission Press.

Serrano, F. L. Personal communications since 2004.

"States' Rights Sustained." *Florida Times-Union* 19 May 1896.

St. Ambrose Centennial Committee. 1975. *The Branches: Springs of Living Water 1875-1975.* Green Cove Springs, Florida: Emerald Printing Company.

St. Augustine Historical Society Research Library.

Ste. Claire, D. 2006. *Cracker: The Cracker Culture in Florida History.* Gainesville, Florida: University Press of Florida.

Stratton, S.A. Personal communications. August 2012.

Waterbury, J. P. 1993. *Coquina.* St. Augustine Historical Society.

# Author Biography

Ann Browning Masters is the author of *Floridanos, Menor-cans, Cattle-Whip Crackers*. Poetry from this collection has been published in anthologies and journals, read at the Marjorie Kinnan Rawlings Annual Conference and Florida Literary Arts Coalition Conferences, recognized at the Florida Folk Festival, and recorded for the Florida State Historical Archives. Dr. Masters is a retired faculty member of St. Johns River State College. She continues to read from her work in the Eckerd College Road Scholar Program. In 2015 she was knighted by the Board of Directors of the Easter Festival Committee of St. Augustine for her dedication in promoting St. Augustine's Spanish heritage. A St. Augustine native, she is a 12th generation Floridian.